Raw Diet for Dogs

Simple Raw Feeding Guide for a Happier Dog

© Copyright 2018 - All rights reserved.

The content contained within this book may not be reproduced, duplicated or transmitted without direct written permission from the author or the publisher.

Under no circumstances will any blame or legal responsibility be held against the publisher, or author, for any damages, reparation, or monetary loss due to the information contained within this book. Either directly or indirectly.

Legal Notice:

This book is copyright protected. This book is only for personal use. You cannot amend, distribute, sell, use, quote or paraphrase any part, or the content within this book, without the consent of the author or publisher.

Disclaimer Notice:

Please note the information contained within this document is for educational and entertainment purposes only. All effort has been executed to present accurate, up to date, and reliable, complete information. No warranties of any kind are declared or implied. Readers acknowledge that the author is not engaging in the rendering of legal, financial, medical or professional advice. The content within this book has been derived from various sources. Please consult a licensed professional before attempting any techniques outlined in this book.

By reading this document, the reader agrees that under no circumstances is the author responsible for any losses, direct or indirect, which are incurred as a result of the use of information contained within this document, including, but not limited to, — errors, omissions, or inaccuracies.

Table Of Contents

Introduction 12

Chapter One: Dog Nutrition-Food and Supplements They Need To Thrive 14

    Water 14

    Proteins 15

    Fat 15

    Vitamins 16

    Minerals 17

    Carbohydrates 17

    Supplements to Consider 18

        Fish Oil 18
        Glucosamine 18
        Probiotics 19
        Multivitamins 20
        Lysine 21
        Milk Thistle 23
        S-Adenosyl Methionine (SAM-e) 24
        Digestive Enzymes 24
        Coenzyme Q10 25
        Azodyl 25

Chapter Two: How to Feed Raw Food to Dogs- Cleaning And Processing 26

    Cleaning and Processing Meats 28

Storing Raw Dog Food..30

Chapter Three: How to Formulate A Diet By Substituting One Protein For Another...... 33

Symptoms of Food Allergies in Dogs.................... 33

Elimination Diet.. 35

Alternate Choices 35

Chapter Four: How To Find Well Sourced Grass-Fed/Pastured Meats For Cheap 37

Natural Food Stores.. 37

Food Co-op 38

Farmer's Market 38

Farm..38

Farm to Door Delivery.. 39

Chapter Five: How to Transition A Dog To Raw Diet..40

Prey Model Raw Diet 40

Starting with the Model..41

Things to Avoid 42

Supplements.. 43

Preparing Bone Broth... 43

BARF Method...44

Why BARF? 45

Issues with BARF 46

How Much to Feed? 47

Switching to BARF 47

Chapter Six: How Much Does It Cost To Follow The Raw Food Diet? 50

Smart Shopping 51

Chapter Seven: Pros and Cons of Adding Vegetables To The Diet............................ 53

Pros of Adding Vegetables.................................... 53
- *Vegetables are Natural Foods................................ 53*
- *Vegetables Alkalize the Body.................................54*
- *Nutritional value..54*
- *Water 54*
- *Vitamins.. 55*
- *Minerals.. 55*
- *Omega-3 .... 55*
- *Phytonutrients.. 56*
- *Enzymes 57*
- *Antioxidants 57*
- *Anti-Inflammatory Molecules 57*
- *Fiber 57*
- *Control diseases 58*

Cons of Feeding Vegetables..................................58
- *Not enough nutrition 58*
- *Toxicity 58*

Chapter Eight: Myths of Raw Feeding 59

Myth 1: Raw Diets aren't Balanced Diets 59

Myth 2: Raw Diets Lead to
Salmonella Infection 60

Myth 3: Raw Diets are Complicated 60

Myth 4: It will be Quite Expensive 61

Myth 5: Raw Diets Make Dogs Aggressive 61

Myth 6: Bones can be Dangerous 62

Myth 7: Raw Meat is Not
Palatable to Small Dogs 62

Chapter Nine: Hacks to Try If Your Dog Hates Certain Raw Foods 64

Adding Raw Goat's Milk to the Meal 64

Krill Oil 64

Switch Up Proteins 65

Heat It 65

Trial and Error 66

Customize 66

Chapter Ten: What to Do When Portions Don't Seem Right Or Your Dog Starts Losing Or Gaining Weight 68

Kicking Off Weight Loss in Dogs 70

Dealing with Weight Loss in Dogs 72

Chapter Eleven: Wide Range of Recommended Sources of Protein for Dogs 73

Chicken and Poultry Meats 75

Other Meats 75

Wrong Protein Choices for Dogs 76

Chapter Twelve: Immunity Boosters For Dogs 78

Fish Oil 78

Vitamin E 78

Rosemary 79

Biotin 79

Coconut Oil 79

Peppermint 80

Plain Yogurt 80

Vitamin C 80

Pumpkin 81

Echinacea 81

Diatomaceous Earth 81

Chapter Thirteen: Types Of Raw Treats For Dogs 83

Lamb Bones 83

Duck Necks 83

Green Tripe 83

Venison Jerky Treats 84

Vegetables 84

Fruits 84

Chapter Fourteen: Tips For Fresher Breath And Cleaner Teeth 85

Probiotics 85

Bones 85

Food 86

Parsley and Mint 86

Coconut Oil 87

Apple Cider Vinegar 87

Natural Treats 87

Chapter: 20 Raw Food Recipes for Dogs .. 89

1. Basic Raw Dog Food 89
   Ingredients: 89
   Method: 90

2. Standard Raw Food for Dogs 91
   Ingredients: 91
   Method: 92

3. Active/Puppy Raw Dog Food 93
   Ingredients: 93
   Method: 93

4. Chicken and Carrots for Beginners 95

Ingredients: 95
Method: 95

5. Beef and Greens for beginners 97
Ingredients: 97
Method: 97

6. Chicken and Greens for beginners 99
Ingredients: 99
Method: 99

7. Turkey and Greens for beginners 101
Ingredients: 101
Method: 101

8. Sweet Turkey for beginners 103
Ingredients: 103
Method: 103

9. Chicken and Beef Delight 105
Ingredients: 105
Method: 105

10. Chicken, Turkey and Fish Delight 107
Ingredients: 107
Method: 107

11. Raw Food Cakes... 109
Ingredients: 109
Method: 111

12. Meat, Fruit and Vegetable Patties................. 113
Ingredients: 113
Method: 113

13. Lamb/Beef, Vegetable and Fruit for Small Breed Dogs up to 17.5 Pounds............................. 115
Ingredients: 115

Method: *116*

14. Beef and Eggs 117
    Ingredients: *117*
    Method: *117*

15. Meatballs 119
    Ingredients: *119*
    Method: *120*

16. Chicken and Fish Exotica 122
    Ingredients: *122*
    Method: *123*

17. Pupcakes – Christmas Pudding for Doggies 124
    Ingredients: *124*
    Method: *124*

18. Fruit Parfait for Dogs 126
    Ingredients: *126*
    Method: *126*

19. Frozen Strawberry and Banana Smoothie Treat 127
    Ingredients: *127*
    Method: *127*

20. Pupsicles 128
    Ingredients: *128*
    Method: *128*

Conclusion 129
References: 130

Introduction

I want to thank you for choosing this book, '*Raw Diet for Dogs: Advanced Guide to Homemade Raw Feeding for a Happier Dog*'

A raw food diet happens to be one of the oldest types of pet foods. There was a time when pet owners did not have access to dog food and relied on whatever was easily available. Even before dogs were domesticated, they relied on raw food for their meals. It is believed that this has conditioned their bodies to accept raw foods and it has not changed over the years.

Pet owners have been investigating the benefits of feeding their dogs raw food for some time now and there have been sufficient studies to prove the various health benefits that it can provide. After all, everyone wants their four-legged family members to live a long and healthy life. In fact, more and more dog owners are now switching over to the raw food diet; as they think it is possible to help their dogs cope better with any existing illnesses and also stave off the occurrence of any future ones.

Apart from illness prevention, raw dog diets can

provide a plethora of other health benefits including: a shinier coat, better digestion, stronger immunity, better health, provide more energy, and increased muscle mass, among others.

If you wish to get your dog on the raw diet, then you have come to the right place! This book will act as your ultimate guide to raw food diet for dogs and how it can be incorporated in your dog's daily diet.

Thank you once again for choosing this book, let's get started.

Chapter One: Dog Nutrition-Food and Supplements They Need To Thrive

In this first chapter, we will look at some supplements required to keep your dog healthy. Here are some important food elements/nutrients to incorporate in your dog's diet:

Water

Water is undoubtedly the most important element that your dog needs to remain healthy. Water is 70% of an adult dog's body mass. Water serves many important functions include dissolving and eliminating toxins from the body and also moving vital nutrients around the body. It also helps to regulate the body temperature while synthesizing the fat and carbohydrates needed to keep up the energy levels. Water helps to provide cushioning for the body and removing waste. The quantity of water your dog needs depends on the amount of activity they get. Most dogs will know exactly how much water to drink, just leaving out a fresh bowl of water will help them get the right amount.

Proteins

Protein is a macronutrient that supplies energy. It helps to supply non-essential amino acids that are required to keep the body healthy. Protein happens to supply the body with a structure such as bones, muscles, and hair. It is also essential for secretion of hormones, enzymes, and antibodies that are needed to keep the body healthy. Dogs have to be exposed to the right amino acids through food. Protein can also supply energy to their bodies if they don't have enough carbohydrates and fats available. The body is incapable of storing proteins and thus requires a constant supply. If you have a puppy or a pregnant dog then they will require twice the proteins as adult dogs. The best source of proteins is meat, eggs, and fish.

Fat

Fat is a macronutrient which gets divided as saturated fat and polyunsaturated fat. Saturated fat is derived from butter and cheese while polyunsaturated fat t is derived from oils and monounsaturated fat. Fat supplies energy in concentration and has two times more calories compared to carbohydrates and proteins. It is important to consume foods that contain Omega 3 and Omega 6 fatty acids, as they help to dissolve vitamins and keep the dog's organs in top shape. Fat also helps to regulate body temperature and promotes a healthy nervous system. Make sure not to overfeed fat to your dog, as it can have a negative effect on his or her body. Flaxseeds, sunflower oil, and olive oil all can be good sources of fat for your dog.

Vitamins

Vitamins are an essential part of the metabolic function and an important part of a dog's diet. Fat soluble vitamins such as A, D, K, and E and water-soluble ones such as B and C are usually stored in the liver and cannot be stored anywhere else in the body, thus there needs to be a constant supply of these vitamins. Vitamins play an important role in regulating the calcium content and phosphorus levels in the body. They are responsible to regularize immunity and to maintain the nervous system function. You have to feed your dog a complete and wholesome diet in order for him or her to receive all the vital vitamins. It should contain both meats and eggs. Make sure you give your dog lots of green leafy vegetables and pure, filtered drinking water.

Minerals

Minerals are inorganic compounds that are required by the body to maintain metabolic function. The body is incapable of producing these and can only be had through food sources. There are two types of minerals in the body: macrominerals and microminerals. They are both equally required by the body to remain healthy. They are a part of bone structure, provide oxygen to the body, help to heal wounds, and regulate fluid balance in the body. Puppies require almost twice as many minerals as adult dogs. Meat is a good source of minerals. Oysters are a great source of iron, copper, manganese, phosphorus, magnesium, selenium, and zinc and are rich in Omega-3 fatty acids as well as Vitamin D.

Carbohydrates

Carbohydrates are macronutrients made of sugar, starches, and fiber that don't get digested by the body. They provide the energy needed by the body to function optimally and are the primary source of glucose, which is required by dogs to have enough energy for carrying out their day-to-day functioning.

Supplements to Consider

Fish Oil

Fish oil is undoubtedly one of the top supplements prescribed for dogs and a very important nutrient to maintain good health. This supplement is usually administered to humans to control the fat levels in the blood and to prevent cardiovascular illnesses; however, this is not primary reason for its use in pets, as they do not suffer from the same type of cardiovascular issues. Instead, it is used to treat skin infections and allergies, which are common in dogs. According to a research, it was found that fish oil supplements can be used to improve the overall coat quality of dogs and decrease the steroidal medications that are required to treat the itching. They also work as a substitute for any of the other therapies that are administered to treat skin allergies.

Another use of fish oil is to treat arthritis in dogs. There is no conclusive evidence to back the theory that fish oil can be an effective treatment for arthritis but it is believed that it can be used to reduce discomfort associated with the condition.

Glucosamine

Glucosamine is another extremely popular supplement for dogs. It is usually administered stand alone, or as a combination with Chondroitin, which is a mussel extract. It can be purchased over the counter or from the veterinarian and is usually added to dog food. Most pet owners feed it to their dogs to prevent osteoarthritis.

Arthritis and osteoarthritis are usually genetic illnesses that many dogs face in their lifetime, especially during old age. It is important to treat it at the earliest stages in order to prevent discomfort. There is no sufficient evidence to prove that glucosamine can be used to treat arthritis.

As per clinical studies in humans, the results failed to be consistent and there was no evidence to prove that it reduced discomfort. It is believed that this might not hold true for pets, especially dogs and cats, and they might experience relief.

Clinical research has shown that glucosamine can be used to treat arthritis in dogs. As per ongoing research, it has been found to be a lot more effective compared to its effects on cats. Veterinarians prescribe it to pet owners to manage arthritis and get some relief from the pain.

Probiotics

Probiotics are just as important for dogs as they are for humans. Although the digestive tracts for the two are very different, probiotics play an important role to maintain your dog's good health. Nobody is completely sure about the different bugs that can be found in the gastrointestinal tract of both humans and dogs. It is a complex structure that influences the flora and can only be restored by introducing Lactobacillus.

As per studies, introducing probiotics can help prevent certain conditions in dogs such as diarrhea and also boost immunity. There is no clinical backing for the same and it is believed that the effects can be quite acute. It was also found that most products did not have accurate labels and did not contain some probiotic bacteria that were mentioned on it. It is therefore best to stick to brands that are genuine and deliver on their promise. Some well-known brands are Royal Canin and Paw Digesticare.

The basic theory behind giving dogs probiotics is that it acts as a supplement for gastrointestinal illnesses. It also helps to maintain the ecosystem within the digestive tract and the gut. Making it a part of your dog's healthcare routine can enhance chances of them maintaining a clean and healthy digestive system.

Multivitamins

As you know, most humans consume multivitamins

in order to fill the gaps left behind by our nutritionally inadequate diets. The same extends to dogs, whose diets might not give them the desired or required doses of vitamins. As per doctors, multivitamins should only be administered upon understanding the deficiencies that are prevalent. Simply administering multivitamins without any evidence of deficiencies will not do any good. In fact, it can sometimes lead to negative consequences.

Administering a healthy diet and incorporating all the necessary nutrients can help prevent the need of giving your dog multivitamins. In fact, it might not be necessary at all. It is best to consult a veterinarian before administering multivitamins; however, it will be quite a compulsory step in case your dog genuinely lacks some vital nutrients such as vitamins and minerals. There is widespread belief that multivitamins are a little harmful in the case of large breed dogs, but there is no scientific backing to support the same. Ensure you read the labels for the contents and consult your veterinarian to understand whether or not the multivitamin is ideal for your dog.

Lysine

Lysine is an important chemical required by pets to produce antibodies. It is an amino acid that should be present in the right quantity, but do you know what these amino acids are? They are chemical compounds and an important part of protein building.

There are two main types of amino acids namely the essential ones and the non-essential ones. The non-essential acids are ones that your pet's body can synthesize from certain elements. The essential ones are those that the body cannot synthesize and have to be added to the body through the consumption of certain foods.

One of the most important amino acids is Lysine. It is recommended to be a part of dog food, as it helps in proper bodily functioning. Lysine helps in the absorption of calcium and promotes proper development of bones. It contributes toward proper maintenance of muscle health and improves the wear and tear of muscles. Lysine helps to fortify the pet's immunity. When consumed with Vitamin C, this amino acid will help to prevent the formation of atheroma plaques, which can lead to a host of cardiovascular issues that are common among dogs.

Some good sources of Lysine are fresh vegetables, dry fruits, eggs, red meats, fish, and poultry. The ideal amount prescribed for adult dogs is about 1 gram per day.

Milk Thistle

Milk thistle is an herb that is recommended for dogs to enhance their good health. Much like glucosamine, it is an element that has moved from conventional medicine and is also used as an alternative medicine.

Milk thistle contains active ingredients known as silymarin. The cluster of compounds has a wide range of benefits and is potentially effective to serve as an anti-inflammatory chemical. It is a form of antioxidant rich compounds that are present in the liver and can work against the metabolism of certain toxic chemicals that are harmful and interfere with the metabolism of certain types of drugs. The chemical has been proven to be effective in stimulating hormones such as estrogen.

The main use of this chemical is to treat any infection or damage to the liver as a result of toxins and other infections and to recover from diabetes and any kidney related issues as a result of toxins. It is usually administered to dogs to treat liver related illnesses. Although there is no concrete proof to prove the effect of this chemical in animals, it is believed that it can lead to considerable decrease in insulin resistance in dogs with diabetes. It can also contribute to a decrease in the lipid levels in blood.

When we consider the risks involved or side effects, there are only a few. Some dogs may suffer from nausea, diarrhea, and other such gastrointestinal illnesses that are common among humans. These can be allergic reactions to the chemicals. It is believed that milk thistle is beneficial in most cases and the harmful effects are rare but not completely impossible to come by.

S-Adenosyl Methionine (SAM-e)

SAM-e is a chemical distributed all throughout the body and comes with an array of in vitro functions. The chemical is promoted for use in humans for treating depression and arthritis. In pets, it is usually used to treat issues related to the liver. It is mostly used in combination with milk thistle in order to treat infections and other issues related to the liver. It's also usually administered to dogs to prevent liver disease and can also be used to treat age related cognitive dysfunction in older dogs.

Digestive Enzymes

Digestive enzymes are extremely important for dogs to maintain a healthy body; however, most of these enzymes are destroyed when the food is processed. This means that most of the nutrients do not make it to the food bowl, as they are killed while being processed. This is exactly why many pet owners turn to raw diet, so that it is easier for the dogs to digest their food.

There have been counter arguments that claim dogs already have the required enzymes in their systems and do not have to turn to food for it. In some studies, these enzymes have been prescribed for the treatment of cancer and can also provide anti-inflammatory effects. They are also recommended for disease control.

Coenzyme Q10

This chemical is usually prescribed for dogs to treat heart related illnesses. It is also prescribed to treat age related cognitive illness. It is said to provide protection against congestive cognitive heart failure.

Azodyl

Azodyl is a mixture of probiotics and prebiotics and is usually prescribed for dogs who have kidney issues. As per research, the idea is to add organisms to the gastrointestinal tract. It can help breakdown nitrogenous wastes that the kidney is responsible for eliminating from the body.

As you can see, there are a lot of nutrients and supplements that are required by your dog to remain healthy. Make sure that you consult a veterinarian to ensure that it is safe to administer these to your dog and there are no negative reactions.

Chapter Two:
How to Feed Raw Food to Dogs- Cleaning And Processing

A lot of people around us are trying their best not to consume processed and junk food. These people have a general healthy attitude towards their diet and lifestyle and the same shows in the way they care for their pets. Many people are trying to keep conventional pet food away from their pets. In doing so, they are turning to old-fashioned ways where the food is raw and unprocessed. This might sound a little strange as many are used to feeding our pets straight from a can, but in doing so, we end up introducing the pet to a whole host of chemicals and bacteria that grow inside the can. This can lead to parasitic illnesses.

Research has shown that raw diets can provide pets with a lot of health benefits that processed food cannot. From improving their overall digestive prowess to providing them with enough nutrition, raw meats can do wonders for your dog. Domestic dogs have evolved no doubt and do not have the same capacity as their wild counterparts. In fact, they have seen about 30,000 years of evolution and their diet is now quite flexible. They can live on a combination of human food and dog food and are also able to digest complex elements such as starch.

Since the olden days, dogs were made to consume raw meats and homemade food. It was not until the early 1900's that processed foods began to be marketed. And although they made several claims and continue to do so, they often fail to deliver on their promise.

Raw diets help keep illnesses related to processed food consumption away and also provide several health benefits. It is important to be a little careful and make sure that you follow the right cleaning and processing techniques before administering the meat to your dogs.

According to a recent study, it was found that out of 35 commercial frozen meats, E. Coli was found in about 28 of them. Listeria monocytogenes was in 19 and salmonella was present in seven. Many of them also were host to certain parasites.

In comparison to this, unprocessed meat that is bought from butchers is less likely to have as many parasites and is a lot safer for raw consumption. But there is not much evidence to prove the same. It is interesting to note that the bacteria and parasites that are usually found in these foods are not really problematic for dogs. Dogs are quite resistant to many bacteria and rarely fall sick, but they are prone to gastric illnesses owing to the consumption of salmonella.

The bigger problem would be dealing with infected dog feces, as it can contain bacteria and spread in humans, which can lead to serious health issues. These infections can be quite difficult to treat as more and more bacteria are becoming antibiotic resistant. It is therefore advisable to ensure that your dog is not infected by any such bacteria via raw meat consumption.

Cleaning and Processing Meats

Although you might not be able to eliminate all the bacteria that might be a part of raw meat, you can always clean and process the meats to eliminate at least a majority of the contaminants. In order to minimize the risk of contamination, try your best to not buy meat from supermarkets. According to recent studies, it was found that these meats could contain high levels of salmonella, as compared to meats found in butcher shops.

Your best option is to go for organic, grass fed meats that contain much less bacteria and will be healthier cuts of meat. Before handling the meat, make sure you wash your hands thoroughly and also clean the surfaces that will come in contact with the raw meat. Make sure you keep the different meats away from each other as mixing them can cause bacteria to transfer.

According to the food safety and inspection service, it is best to wash your hands for at least 20 seconds before and after handling meats. The cutting boards and utensils should be washed in hot soapy water after each use. The countertops have to be cleaned with hot soapy water after the meats have been placed on them.

The best and most effective way to defrost or thaw meats is by placing them in sealed containers inside the refrigerator until it rises to a normal temperature.

Make sure you sterilize all the equipment including pet bowls. Invest in high quality bowls that are resistant to bacteria.

If you suspect that your dog has been exposed to harmful bacteria, then take him to the vet immediately.

The harmful bacteria can be passed on to humans via feces, and exposed surfaces such as beds, couches, and toys. They can also be passed on by touching and petting dogs and coming in contact with floors and toys that they have been using.

Make sure you encourage your dog to defecate outside the house and use gloves or poop scoopers to pick up the waste. Always wash your hands with hot water and use an antiseptic soap to kill the germs. Encourage your children to do the same. Never eat without washing your hands, especially after petting the dog.

Storing Raw Dog Food

If you wish to store your dog's raw food then you have to more or less follow the same principles as storing your own food such as chicken and other meats. All you have to do is add it to good quality plastic containers or Ziploc bags and place it in the freezer. This can prevent the formation of harmful bacteria on the meats. The temperature inside the freezer has to be maintained at about 0 degrees F in order to keep bacteria from forming on the meats. It will also keep other microbes such as mold and yeast in control and slow down the activity associated with enzymes that can activate in the meats.

In fact, it is not just the meats that need to be stored properly; vegetables and fruits also develop mold and bacteria over time. Freezing them is the best ways to keep them clean. Divide the meats into portions and place them in boxes and bags that mention the expiry dates for the meats.

In general, raw meats that are frozen correctly can last up to 3 months. If you wish to store the raw foods in the refrigerator then maintain the temperatures below 40 degrees F. According to food experts, bacteria can grow between 40 - 140 degrees F. As little as 20 minutes can be enough for the bacteria to double in quantity. Make it a point to maintain the temperatures below 40 degrees F to protect the food.

If by chance the temperature ends up going above 40 degrees for more than two hours, then it is best to get rid of the meat altogether. The best way to tell if meat has gone bad is by inspecting its color and texture. If it has gone pale blue, green and has a slimy texture then get rid of it immediately and wash your hands. It will also smell awful and produce a rancid stink.

Defrosting should be done the right way by taking the meats outside the freezer or fridge and left out until the meat thaws. Make sure to defrost only one or two servings of meat.

Teach your children the importance of storing and serving raw food the right way. Have them observe you when you do it so that they learn the right techniques. Supervise them when they feed dogs raw foods.

Chapter Three:
How to Formulate A Diet By Substituting One Protein For Another

When it comes to the raw diet, it is important to note that your dog might not be able to consume everything that you give him. His body might not be accustomed to all the foods that you put on his plate.

Many pet owners often fail to understand that some dogs can't digest certain proteins such as beef and chicken. They can suffer from diarrhea and inflammation of the anal glands. This can lead to discomfort and a feeling of uneasiness. In such a case, it becomes important to identify the ingredients that your dog is allergic to and how you can eliminate them from the diet.

Symptoms of Food Allergies in Dogs

The following are some symptoms that your dog might display if he or she is allergic to certain foods. This list has been formulated based on feedback from pet owners and veterinarians

- Itchy paws. You will find your pooch constantly licking his or her paws and scratching them

- Loud noises in the stomach that sound like gurgling noises

- Diarrhea and loose stools and an urge to defecate several times a day

- Flatulence. Often smelly gas that does not leave the room easily

- Anal gland failure that makes it difficult for your dog to eliminate waste

- Infections inside the ear

- Rashes and hives that form on the skin and flaky skin

- Hair falling off in patches

- Constant nausea

- Laziness

These happen to be just some symptoms that might be apparent if your dog is allergic to certain foods. If you spot any of these and it stays for more than a week then your dog might have a food allergy.

Elimination Diet

In order to know what is troubling your dog's digestive system, you have to engage in elimination diet. It is one where you remove a certain ingredient from the diet to check whether it is the cause for your dog's discomfort.

For example, if you feed them turkey and beef then eliminate the turkey for one week and check if there is an improvement in the symptoms. If there isn't then add turkey back to their diet and eliminate the beef. You will notice that there is an improvement in the symptoms. Once you feel the symptoms have completely disappeared, you can introduce another meat as a substitute for beef. Go for chicken or ham. But again, test it out for one week to make sure the new meat is palatable.

Sometimes, it might take longer than a week for the symptoms to appear and disappear. Try to extend the elimination period to a month. One such ingredient happens to be beef tripe. It might take longer for the symptoms to go away. It usually causes skin issues, diarrhea and gurgling sounds in the stomach along with ear infections.

Alternate Choices

If you notice that your dog is allergic to beef and

chicken then it is best to add alternate meats to the diet. In doing so, make sure you only introduce small quantities. Do not overload your pet with new foods, as it can lead to gastrointestinal issues.

Alternatives to chicken and beef include pheasant, emu, turkey, rabbit, lamb, duck, and elk. These will be easier to find at co-ops as compared to other proteins.

Note that if your dog is allergic to beef then chances are high he is also allergic to venison, bison and buffalo meat. So, try to eliminate these from the diet to ensure that the allergens are dealt with.

If your dog is allergic to lamb meat then chances are he is also allergic to turkey, duck and eggs. Many dogs will be allergic to eggs and can develop skin issues. It is important to make sure that you introduce organic grass-fed meats. We will look at how you can find the right sources in the next chapter.

Chapter Four: How To Find Well Sourced Grass-Fed/Pastured Meats For Cheap

If you are wondering where you can find well sources grass fed meats for cheaper then here is a simple guide to follow to know exactly where to look for them.

Natural Food Stores

One of the best options to find well-sourced grass fed meats are natural food stores. They stock pasteurized meats. All you have to do is ask the butcher present a few simple questions to know whether it is organic or grass fed meat. Questions include: Where do the meats come from? How were the animals raised? What type of diet were the animals fed? Were they allowed to graze freely in the open? Answers to these will tell you whether or not the animals are grass fed.

Food Co-op

A food co-op refers to a food club where customers are made to buy products in bulk at cheaper rates compared to natural food stores. These co-ops only entertain people who are members. They will collect an initial bulk sum to set up the co-op and then provide great discounts to the members. Look up one such co-op in your area and get the best wholesale rates.

Farmer's Market

Farmer's markets happen to be great sources to find organic, grass fed meats. If you are looking for special cuts and organic meats then they are great to consider. Find one in your area and if there isn't one then consider looking for an online store.

Farm

It might seem next to impossible to find farms in your area but you might stumble upon a small one on the outskirts of your city. If you do find one then ask them the same questions as you would ask your natural food store butcher to know about the meats. You can also observe them yourselves to know how they are being raised. It is also easy to find meats on online sites such as eatwild.com and eatlocalgrown.com. Once you find the list of farms that look genuine, email them or call them to enquire about the meats and their quality.

Farm to Door Delivery

Last but not the least, look for a farm to door delivery service that will deliver the meats straight to your doorstep. They can make it easier for you to find pasteurized meats that are delivered right to your doorstep. Look up for such a service in your area. Make sure you read their testimonials to know whether they are reliable. Right from grass fed steak to free range chicken, they can provide you with many types of organic, grass fed meats.

As you can see, there are quite a few choices to consider when it comes to finding organic meats. Do not give into the temptation of going for supermarket meats as they will not be healthy and can contain harmful bacteria.

Chapter Five: How to Transition A Dog To Raw Diet

When it comes to transitioning your dog to the raw diet there are a few models to be considered. They are as mentioned below.

Prey Model Raw Diet

The prey model raw diet is all about feeding meats, bones and other organs in the ratio 80:10:5:5. The muscle meat ratio should make up for 80% of the diet followed by 10% bone content followed by 5% liver and 5% other organs such as kidney, heart etc.

The idea is to maintain this ratio so that it is easier to calculate and feed your dog. Don't worry if the ratios are not perfect, it can be a near accurate guess. The important bit is to be able to provide healthy, organic meat free of chemicals and loaded with vitamins and minerals. Try to mix up the meat by switching one type of meat that is tolerated by your dog to another kind to make sure your dog gets all the vital nutrients.

If you are going for fresh meat that has just been hunted down then it has to be frozen for three weeks at least to kill parasites and bacteria.

A good bowl of prey model diet consists of ground beef, Blue Ridge beef with a mix of liver, kidney, tripe, pork neck, coconut oil and bone broth. Throw in some herbs to make it a little healthier.

Starting with the Model

If you are interested in helping your dog switch to the prey model then there are some healthy methods to do so. One of the best ways is to use simple meat such as chicken breast ground to a mince. Give it to your dog for one week and then gradually mix in organs and bones over the course of the next two weeks. Be prepared for episodes of diarrhea, as it is not easy for dogs to adjust to a raw diet. This phase of loose stools is better known as the "detox" phase. It is when the body gets rid of any food that has been over processed. Once the body is back to normal, go ahead and add in new proteins to their diet such as beef and ham.

If you think your dog is having extended periods of loose stools then consider giving them more calcium so that it can combine with the stools and solidify. But make sure you do not overfeed them bones as it can lead to very hard stools.

You might have to engage in a little trial and error to come up with the right ratios but will be well worth it as you will know exactly how much to feed your dog to keep him healthy and happy. Don't worry if you end up over feeding or under feeding them, once you know exactly how much food they need, you will be able to make the adjustments.

If your dog is used to consuming kibble then start off on the raw diet by adding in a little ground meat to their kibble. Increase the raw meat gradually while decreasing the kibble. Keep at it until all the kibble has been replaced with the raw meat.

Do not forget to give them raw fish, as it is important for them to get the required nutrients from fish. Salmon fillets and whole tilapia happen to be good options.

Things to Avoid

Try not to mix kibble and meats on bones all at once. There is belief that the two will not go well together and can lead to stomach issues and blockages. So, it is best to keep them separate and not mix them in the same bowl. If you are going for fish, then go for fresh caught fish and not farm raised ones. The latter might not be raised in the best of conditions. Try not to give your dogs heavy and thick bones that are quite hard. They can end up breaking or splintering your dog's teeth.

Supplements

It is obvious that the diet alone might not be able to provide all the necessary nutrients. It is therefore best to add in a few supplements that can make up for the missing nutrients. A good multivitamin can do the trick. Ask the veterinarian first to make sure the multivitamin is palatable. Try to rotate the proteins in the diet to make sure a variety of nutrients are provided. One of the best and wholesome meals for your dog is bone broth which is made by simmering raw bones for 18 o 24 hours in a crockpot and contains tons of vitamins and nutrients that can enhance immunity. Bone broth usually contains multivitamins such as Vitamin C, D, K, iron, Thiamin, calcium, potassium, silicon, magnesium, sulphur, and many other vital nutrients.

Preparing Bone Broth

It is very easy to make bone broth. All you have to do is add some raw bones to a crock-pot along with enough water to cover the bones and a tablespoon of apple cider vinegar. This is done to bring out more nutrients from the bones. Simmer it for 18 to 24 hours. Once done, it will store well in glass jars for about two weeks in the fridge. Try to get rid of the fat that forms on top. Do not give your dogs the cooked bones at any cost. They can be quite hard and end up causing injury.

The prey model is an easy one to follow as it is quite simple to come up with the ratios and you will feel satisfied knowing you are feeding your dog a wholesome meal. You must ideally feed them 2 to 3% of their body weight. But it will also depend on their rate of metabolism.

Make sure you are constantly in touch with the vet and take your dog for regular check-ups. You have to do what is right for your pet and his needs.

BARF Method

The next method is known as the BARF method. It stands for bones and raw food or biologically appropriate raw food. Ian Billinghurst, an Australian vet, started the method. He promoted the method as being one of the best to consider for dogs and cats as it taps into their natural instincts.

As per Billinghurst, dogs are only used to consuming processed foods for over 80 years now, meaning, their digestive systems have not evolved to accept the change as yet. It is therefore important to take them back to their natural foods in order to ensure that their digestive systems go back to normalcy.

He therefore advocated feeding dogs with meaty bones and raw vegetables and cutting out all forms of carbohydrates.

Why BARF?

As you know, it is important to feed dogs a wholesome diet consisting of nutrients that are vital for their growth and development. Commercial products will not have enough nutrients and can be quite starchy and sugary. They can also end up having allergens that can negatively impact your dog's health.

In such a case, shifting your dog to a raw diet can help them reel in good health.

Switching to the BARF diet can help you address some issues such as helping them live a longer and healthier life.

Here are some advantages associated with this diet

- It can lead to the development of leaner and stronger muscles
- It can reduce the number of allergies
- It can produce firmer stools

- It will keep your dog's teeth clean
- It helps to develop muscles
- It can decrease body odor
- It is a natural source of minerals and calcium
- It can help to enhance your dog's coat
- The diet can help your dog live a longer life
- You will be able to help your dog manage his weight better

Issues with BARF

BARF is not fully supported by the pet owner's community, as there still remain some concerns over the legitimacy of the diet. Some issues are as follows:

- Feeding dogs bones that are too hard can cause them injury
- Raw meats can make dogs quite aggressive
- Raw meats can contain a lot of parasites and bacteria
- Raw foods can lead to diarrhea, constipation, and vomiting

However, these are mere myths and will not hold true in a majority of cases. We will be busting most of these myths in a future chapter.

How Much to Feed?

As mentioned earlier, how much food your dog needs depends on his body weight and activity level. But to make it a bit easier for you to know the exact ratio, it is best to give your dog one pound of BARF for every fifty pounds of dog weight.

Give them this amount for at least a month to know whether you are feeding the right amount. You might have to adjust this amount a little to hit the right ratio. Keep track of your dog's weight to ensure it is not drastically increasing or decreasing.

Most pet owners feed their dogs the BARF diet twice a day but you can feed it to them thrice a day if you wanted to. The morning meal is usually made up of meaty bones and the evening meals are made of vegetables and ground meat. If you have a puppy, pregnant, or lactating female then the ratio has to be much higher.

Switching to BARF

When it comes to transitioning your dog to the BARF diet, it is best to go with the cold turkey method. It is one where you switch up your dog's diet drastically by giving them raw foods in place of their regular foods. You do not slowly transition them and instead give them raw foods out of the blue. This might sound a little controversial and even shocking but can be an effective method to get their bodies to adjust to the diet faster.

They will experience episodes of loose stools, vomiting, and constipation but nothing that cannot be fixed within a week or two. If they have it for longer then switch up the meats to check if they are intolerant to some foods. They might be allergic to nuts, seeds, meats, and even certain vegetables. It will be important to give them supplements to make up for any nutritional deficiencies in their meals.

Many people give their dogs ground up bones. This might lead to some issues such as lacerations in the mouth. It would therefore be best to give them whole bones instead of grinding them up. Remember to be by your dog's side when you give them the raw diet. It will help **them** adjust to the diet in a better way knowing you are by their side to lend emotional support.

Try out a simple method where you maintain a base meat that your dog can tolerate such as chicken or ham and keep switching up the second meat. Grind up meat to make it easier for your dog to eat. Lamb and beef usually go well with chicken.

Some people give their dog the raw food on alternate days for a week to help the food digest properly. It will also allow their bodies' time to adjust to the new diet.

To make it easier, do not give your dog vegetables for the first few days and weeks. Avoid supplements too so that it is not over burdening. Give them yogurt as it contains a lot of antibiotics that can help maintain a healthy digestive system.

Once your dog's digestive system is well adjusted, add raw meats with bones and necks and wings etc. It is ideal to serve minced meats at nights to make it easier for them to digest it. Slowly introduce vegetables by giving them about 4 tablespoons per day. Consider mixing it in with the meat, as many dogs do not like having vegetables. Introduce supplements slowly tablespoon by tablespoon. It is recommended to give them vitamins C and E.

In about a month's time your dog will be ready for raw bones. Go for smaller ones at first before giving them beef knuckles and lamb legs. Usually, it takes no more than a month for dogs to adjust to the BARF diet. Both the methods are easy to follow. Choose whichever method is best suited for your dog.

Chapter Six: How Much Does It Cost To Follow The Raw Food Diet?

When it comes to adopting a new method, one of the first things that concern people is the cost of the diet. It is essential to calculate the cost first to ensure that you are prepared for the financial liability. In order to know the costs, you must calculate your own estimate. Here is how you can do so.

For a majority of dogs, it is best to feed them 2 to 3% of their body weight. But this will differ based on their activity levels. For example, dogs who are couch potatoes might need much less compared to more active dogs.

In order to know how much to feed, simply multiply your dog's current weight by 0.02 or 0.03. Once you have the number, divide it by two or three depending on the number of meals you wish to feed them per day.

If you are measuring it is pounds then the weight of food will be in pounds, if you are using kilograms then the weight of food will be in kilograms and so on.

If your dog weighs 50 lb then 2% will be 1 lb per day and 30 lb per month. 80% has to be muscles, 10% bones, 5% liver and 5% other organs. It can also include vegetables, dairy and so on.

Based on this, you will able to calculate the daily and monthly costs. It is understood that it can seem a little expensive as you will have to pay a little extra for meat that is sourced from farms and natural food stores. But it will be well worth it, as your dog will have access to healthier ingredients.

Smart Shopping

Engaging in some smart shopping can help you save on quite a few dollars. Although this will need some extra work, it can help you save big. Costs will obviously vary from place to place. You have to find out where it is cheaper and where it is a little more expensive. But that does not mean you compromise on the quality.

Clean, hygienic grocery stores can have chicken wings, legs and gizzards at reasonable prices. There might be offers running so make sure you ask about them before buying.

Specialty food stores such as Chinese, Asian, and

Mexican will always have a variety of foods on offer at reasonable rates. They usually sell organ meats and might also have gizzards. Most of these places will have fish that is fresher than what you would find at large grocery stores and deli sections.

Although rabbit and quail meat will be a little more expensive than other proteins, consider buying them once in a while to introduce a little variety in your dog's diet. But make sure they can tolerate these.

As discussed in a previous chapter, it is always best to go for co-ops. They will give you the best deals and offers. You can save on quite a bit of money on a monthly basis. They usually buy in bulk. This will benefit the members. But the only issue is that you will have to buy the products in bulk. You will have to buy it in 30 to 50 pounds boxes. So, unless you are good at storing food the correct way, it is best to buy in smaller quantities.

The best way to store it will be in heavy-duty freezers. Buy a good freezer where the meats can be stored and preserved for longer.

If you have the means for it, then consider having a farm of your own. Raising chicken and goats can help you have a consistent, fresh supply of raw meat for your dog.

Chapter Seven: Pros and Cons of Adding Vegetables To The Diet

When it comes to the raw diet for dogs, it is important not to make it only about meats and non vegetarian foods. You must introduce some vegetables as well so that it is easier to fill the gaps left behind by non veg food.

Pros of Adding Vegetables

Vegetables are Natural Foods

Dogs have not evolved as yet to be completely dependent on meats alone. There was a time when they were wild animals who consumed whatever was available to them. This included vegetables and fruits. They are usually not obligated to consume meats alone and so, it would be best to introduce some vegetables into their raw food diet. In fact, dogs have consumed all types of vegetables for hundreds of years and thus their guts and livers will be able to process them well. Start small. Give them smaller portions of the vegetables. Don't go in for too much at once as it can end up confusing their systems. If you are starting them on the raw diet then introduce the vegetables step by step over a two- or three-week period.

Vegetables Alkalize the Body

It is important to balance out the acidity and alkalinity in your dog's stomach to ensure that optimum health is maintained. Many of their vital organs will function well in an alkaline environment including gallbladder, hormones, kidneys, and pancreas. If there is too much acidity then it can lead to inflammation and chronic illnesses. Proteins such as meats tend to make their bodies more acidic and vegetables can lead to an alkalizing effect.

Nutritional value

Vegetables lend the body with proteins, fats, carbs and phytonutrients, which makes them super foods. They also lend fiber, which is essential to keep the digestive tract clean and well functioning. Larger dogs might need some extra help keeping their systems clean so introducing a larger portion of vegetables might be necessary.

Water

As mentioned in the first chapter, the most vital aspect of your dog's nutrition is water. Water has a lot of minerals and vitamins that are responsible for keeping your dog healthy and well hydrated. Vegetables and fruits are natural sources of water. By feeding them these, you push chances of them getting the recommended dose and developing a healthy body. There will be decreased chances of them developing kidney and bladder issues.

Vitamins

Raw vegetables provide a whole host of vitamins that are important to keep your dog healthy. Some of them include Vitamins B, E, and C. B vitamins such as thiamine and choline might be missing but these are usually added via meats and bones. Vitamin C is usually produced in the body but they will need it to remain healthy. Vitamins A, E, and K will help them live a healthy life.

Minerals

Minerals are vital for your dog's body and dark leafy vegetables are loaded with some essential ones such as potassium, magnesium, and calcium. Vegetables such as seaweed and alfalfa are great additions as they go deep within the soil and absorb many nutrients that are beneficial. But be sure to only buy organic ingredients and stay away from GMO ones.

Omega-3

Omega 3 is an essential nutrient that should be a

part of your dog's diet. It consists of essential fatty acids that are required to keep their bodies healthy. Omega 3 fatty acids also help to reduce inflammation and support brain function and keep the central nervous system healthy. It also aids in digestion and enhancing immune function. Omega 3 is also used to assist with reproduction. Sometimes, dogs tend to have a lot of Omega 6 in their system, which has to be balanced out with Omega 3. Plant based Omega 3 is always better than fish oil-based Omega 3 fatty acids as the latter can turn rancid quite fast. Omega 3 fatty acids help to impair degeneration in dogs and also slow down aging.

Phytonutrients

Phytonutrients are compounds that are only found in vegetables and not meats. They are chemicals that provide protective enzymes and antioxidants to the body. They also have anti-inflammatory properties that make them ideal for controlling inflammation in the dog's body. Phytonutrients have other beneficial properties such as antiviral, antifungal, and anthelmintic properties. If you feed your dog with just kibble then they will not get any of these nutrients.

Enzymes

Enzymes that are part of vegetables are required to keep the digestive system healthy. Fruits, such as pineapple have bromelain and papaya, which has papain, are healthy options. Some enzymes are able to move past the acid produced in the stomach and will be fully absorbed by the body. When this happens, they will provide anti-aging benefits that will keep your dog's body healthy.

Antioxidants

Vegetables and fruits are full of antioxidants that are required to disable oxidative damage. They protect against free radicals that lead to aging and other illnesses. It is therefore essential to give your dogs fruits and vegetables.

Anti-Inflammatory Molecules

Inflammation can lead to complications and thus should be controlled. Anti-inflammatory molecules can control inflammation to a large extent. They can be derived from spices such as turmeric and herbs such as rosemary. Berries also are a good source of anti-inflammatory molecules.

Fiber

Healthy fiber is required to keep your dog healthy. It is an essential part of keeping the digestive tract free from blockages and smooth running. Vegetables contain fiber that helps to put the digestive tract into overdrive and keep blockages in control. Fiber is especially important in controlling degeneration in older dogs.

Control diseases

Vegetables can control the onset of diseases. They can control and treat illnesses such as kidney, heart disease and cancer.

Cons of Feeding Vegetables

Not enough nutrition

As you know, vegetables will not be able to provide all the required nutrients single-handedly. They will have to be supplemented with meats. Your dog will not do well if he is given just a vegetarian diet. It will not prove to be nourishing enough. Apart from meats, you must also add in legumes, nuts, and seeds in order to balance out the amino acids.

Toxicity

Some vegetables can be toxic when fed in raw form. These include potatoes, tomato plants, mushrooms and many others that should never be fed raw.

Chapter Eight: Myths of Raw Feeding

It is obvious that there area few myths surrounding the raw diet for dogs. In this chapter, we will bust some of them.

Myth 1: Raw Diets aren't Balanced Diets

One of the biggest myths surrounding the raw diet is that people tend to think it is not wholesome or a balanced diet. That it will not be able to provide all the requisite nutrition for your dog. But this is not true. It might be true only if you end up giving your dog just one type of meat or one type of vegetable. But providing a balanced diet consisting of meats and vegetables along with legumes, nuts, and seeds can help you dog get a large portion of the recommended nutrients. Adding in bones to the mix makes it even healthier. It will also provide the essential fatty acids required to keep them healthy along with vitamins and minerals.

Myth 2: Raw Diets Lead to Salmonella Infection

One of the biggest health scares associated with the raw diet is that people think it can lead to salmonella and other bacterial infections. But the truth is, your dog's systems are capable of handling a little salmonella infestation. Their bodies will produce antibodies that will destroy them in no time. It will only be a problem if they are exposed to meat that is heavily infested.

Dogs have natural enzymes and highly acidic stomachs that are more than capable of destroying salmonella and other such bacteria. But it would be best to make sure that there is none on the raw meat you feed them and wash your hands thoroughly before and after handling their meat.

Remember that canned food can contain more salmonella than raw foods. It is therefore important to be more worried about the hygiene associated with feeding them canned food.

Myth 3: Raw Diets are Complicated

This is not true at all! If you are thinking of feeding your dog a raw diet then it is quite easy to calculate the portions. As mentioned earlier, calculating the amount of food to give your dog can be quite just by following the 80:10:5:5 rule.

And it is not important for you to reach out for weaponry and go hunting for the prey to feed your dog. Looking for a good farm that provides healthy, grass fed produce is enough to keep your dog healthy. And there is no need to engage in cooking, as everything will be fed raw.

Myth 4: It will be Quite Expensive

Again, this is just an assumption. If you are moving your dog from kibble to raw food, then it might actually help you save some money. Going for cheaper cuts of meats will make it easier for you to cut down on some costs of feeding your dog. Going for gizzard and bones will considerably lower costs. Look for a butcher in your area who can provide cheaper cuts of meat.

Myth 5: Raw Diets Make Dogs Aggressive

This is another classic myth associated with the raw diet. Many believe that it can make dogs a lot more aggressive if you feed them raw meats. But this is not true. This thought stems from the fact that the blood content in the meat will lead to bloodlust. But this fear is unwarranted. There are no studies to prove the same. If your dog is showing aggression then it can mean he is getting a little territorial with his food. He might need a little training to make him less territorial and more acceptable to people approaching his food.

Myth 6: Bones can be Dangerous

This is partially true, in that, it is important to find bones that are not too hard or too soft. Small, fine bones might get stuck in their systems and might have to be flushed out. Big, tough bones can be quite difficult for them to chew and break down. But it is imperative to provide them with bones, as it will keep their bones healthy and strong. It will also keep their teeth clean and strong. It is a good idea to consider giving them bone broth as opposed to bones themselves.

Myth 7: Raw Meat is Not Palatable to Small Dogs

There is a misconception that a raw diet is only suitable for large dogs and smaller breeds will not be able to adjust to it. But this is not true. It does not depend on the size of the breed. A small breed like Chihuahua will be able to digest raw meat just as well as a Saint Bernard. The trick is to feed them the right amount of meat. This will depend on the size of the dogs. It might be important to give them smaller sized bones or grind them up to make it easier for them to consume them. Just make sure you transition smaller breeds into raw diets in a smooth way.

Chapter Nine: Hacks to Try If Your Dog Hates Certain Raw Foods

It is obvious that your dog is not going to like everything you feed him. They can be quite choosy, especially if they have been fed kibble all their life. In such a case, it can pay to try out a few hacks to get them to eat what you want them to.

Adding Raw Goat's Milk to the Meal

A neat trick that many pet owners use to get their dogs to try out a new food is by adding goat's milk to the mix. Dogs love the taste of raw milk and will almost always eat when it is added in to their meals. It is full of nutrients such as vitamin B6, calcium, proteins, and potassium. It is much better than cow's milk as it is lower in sugar content and has almost two times the Vitamin A. Simply add in half a cup of goat's milk to their meal.

Krill Oil

Krill oil is more or less like fish oil in terms of the taste and smell and is sure to get your dog to eat the meal. In fact, he will be more than willing to have a go considering the appetizing taste. But remember that the oil can be much more potent than fish oil so be sure to use only a little amount. It is rich in antioxidants that can provide multiple benefits to your dog. Krill oil will help to keep your dog's heart and brain healthy. It is also a better option to fish oil, as it will contain lesser levels of mercury and other metals and toxins.

Switch Up Proteins

Dogs will not like it if you keep giving them the same proteins day in day out. If you add a new ingredient in then it will raise their curiosity and they will eat the raw meal without a fuss. It is believed that most dogs are open to eating a meal if organ meat is added in. So chop up some livers and kidneys and add it in so that it makes it interesting for them. Some pet owners also add in an entire egg to the mix to get their dogs to have the meal.

Heat It

Now this might sound very strange, as the whole concept of raw diets is to do with feeding your dogs raw meats. But heating up does not have to mean cooking it. Your dog might not like cold raw meat, especially in the mornings. If you have a picky dog then consider heating it up just so that it stops being cold and reaches room temperature. It has to be warm to the touch and not too hot. The ideal way to do this is by placing the meat in a deep bowl and pouring hot water over it. Allow it to thaw and reach room temperature before feeding it to your dog.

Trial and Error

Engaging in some level of trial and error will be necessary to know exactly what to give your dog and how much. It is impossible to know what they will go for and what they will want to avoid if they have never been fed raw meat before. So make a little effort in maintaining a diary and recording information about their likes and dislikes so that you know what to feed them. As per experts, if you make the meal look a little interesting, such as experiment with the shape or texture then your dog is more likely to consume the meal.

Customize

Customize a meal plan specific to your dog's particular breed. If you go by the book or what other people are feeding their dogs then your dog might not enjoy his meals. In fact, it might turn out to be a big challenge as some dogs do not do well with certain meats and might end up becoming sick. So, talk with the vet and customize a plan to include foods that he is likely to eat and then introduce a new ingredient every now and then to cater to their taste.

Chapter Ten: What to Do When Portions Don't Seem Right Or Your Dog Starts Losing Or Gaining Weight

When it comes to the raw diet, the nutrition content will be much different from the content found in kibble. One of the prominent features of a raw diet is that it is much lower in calories compared to canned food diet. This means that you will surely notice a change in your dog's weight when you feed him a raw diet. The diet helps to reset the biological functioning of your dog and enhances metabolism. This makes it easier for their bodies to absorb the various nutrients much easily and develop a healthy body.

Some people might think of this as a negative thing as they are used to seeing their dogs being overweight—which starts to look like a healthy aspect after a prolonged time. But it is important to understand that being fat does not equate to being healthy. If your dog starts to lose weight and reaches his or her ideal weight then it means the diet has worked well and is helping them remain healthy. If you feel like their weight is going below the ideal limit then it is best to have it checked by a vet to find the issue.

One thing to note is that it is also possible for your dog to gain excess weight by following the raw diet. If you overfeed them not knowing how much they should be ideally eating then they will develop large bodies and want to keep eating all the time.

So, the best thing to do is make use of the calculator that was discussed in a previous chapter. The 2% and 3% rule will always help you know exactly how much food your dog needs to remain healthy and neither gain too much weight or lose too much weight. They will remain at their ideal weight.

Here are three mistakes to avoid when calculating the amount of food required by your dogs.

- Make sure you are using the meal calculator the right way. It is essential to get the ratio right. Weigh your dogs from time to time to make sure you know their exact weight and then do the calculations. Keep yourself motivated to carry out this procedure regularly so that you know exactly how much to feed and do not overfeed or under feed your dog

- Catering to your dog's specific needs is quite important. You have to give them the raw food based on how much they can eat and how much is palatable to them. It might be 2% for some and 3% for others. The types of proteins should also be customized to suit their individual requirements

- Monitor their weight every week as soon as you put them on the raw diet. This will help you keep track of any of the changes in their weight and body mass

Kicking Off Weight Loss in Dogs

It is important for pet owners to treat obesity as an issue and jump-start the weight loss process in dogs. But it is important to go about it the right way to make sure that your dog loses weight holistically.

There are many controversial solutions that are advertised including weight loss pills and supplements that are said to help dogs lose weight. But these pills and supplements might not deliver on their promise and end up being placebos or mere experiments.

The best way to get your dog to lose weight is by following the same principles that apply to humans, which is to restrict the number of calories consumed by the dog and increase the level of exercise.

Here are tips to kick-start their weight loss.

- A neat trick to increase their rate of metabolism is by adding some fish oil to their meals. Adding raw fish to their meals is also a good way to start the process. Raw sardines, canned sardines, and fish oil can be alternated to introduce variety.

- If you have access to pure virgin coconut oil then that too will do the trick. MCT oil is also a good choice and will not only kick start metabolism but also increase your dog's energy and offset weight loss. Coconut oil can also be used to start off the weight loss journey. The ideal amount of oil to add is one teaspoon for every ten pounds body weight. So, if your dog weighs 50 lbs then add five teaspoons of oil to their meal

- A big mistake to avoid is not giving them enough nutrients to maintain consistent energy levels. Losing weight does not mean cutting out the requisite calories needed to carry out day-to-day activities. The lack of calories can make them listless and unable to carry out any physical exercises. To solve this issue, add a little green tripe to the mix so that they get their ideal level of calories and can be active and energetic all day

- Get yourself a good quality food weighing scale that can be used to weigh all the foods that you plan to feed your dog. This includes the bones, muscle meat, organ meat, supplements etc.

Dealing with Weight Loss in Dogs

If you suspect your dog is losing weight on the diet then it is best to feed them certain ingredients that are healthy and interesting so that they feel the urge to finish their entire bowl. Some of these ingredients include raw eggs, raw sardines, bone broth, goat's milk, kefir lime peels, and meaty bones. Add in chopped sweet vegetables such as carrots or beetroots for some variety.

Chapter Eleven: Wide Range of Recommended Sources of Protein for Dogs

All pet owners want their dogs to be strong and healthy. For this, it is important to feed them proteins that are ideal for their bodies and will help to develop strong muscles and bones.

Proteins make up a very important part of any dog's diet. Without proteins, dogs cannot lead a healthy life. If your dogs lack proteins then some symptoms include:

- Lower levels of energy
- Lethargy
- Weight gain
- Skin issues
- Dull coat and shedding
- Behavioral issues
- Weaker bones and deformities

- Wounds healing slowly
- Weak immune system

When it comes to the proteins to feed your dog, it is not about what they want to eat as much as it is about what their bodies can digest. You must go for proteins that have a high biological value. These refer to those that are easy to digest. Meats with low biological values refer to those whose protein content is not easily absorbed by your dog's body. It will simply go through the body without being used and get pushed out. Proteins with high biological values will be easily broken down and absorbed by your dog's body and lead to stronger muscles and bones.

The best source of proteins has to be meats. Although plants too provide protein content, it is inferior to the protein provided by meats. So, if you want your dog to have better access to proteins with higher biological values then it is best to go for meats. Real meats such as chicken, fish, and liver are the best to go for. They will contain superior levels of protein and are easily digested by dogs. The meats are palatable and come from all the best sources.

Here is a list of meats that are best to consider for your dog

Chicken and Poultry Meats

Chicken and poultry meats are for the best sources of proteins for dogs. They can be low in fat content and high-quality proteins capable of keeping your dog healthy and energetic all day. These proteins are easily digested and processed quickly. Poultry meats include the likes of turkey and duck meat. Fish is also a great source of protein for dogs. It contains Omega 3 fatty acids, which is a healthy source of fat required to keep their hearts healthy and also lend their coats a healthy sheen.

Other Meats

Apart from chicken and poultry meats, some other good quality meats to feed your dog include venison, beef, and livers. They are full of healthy proteins that are good for your dog.

Meat meals also happen to be good options. Meat meals refer to meats whose water content is dried in order to leave behind just protein rich meats. They are often referred as meat by products. Chicken meat meals can provide your dog with all the requisite proteins to keep him healthy. But do not mistake these for meat by products, as they are not the same thing. The high-quality concentrated protein content means you do not have to give them a large quantity and limit it to just a small portion. Some high-quality meat meal options include chicken meal, lamb meal, duck meal, turkey meal, buffalo meal, and beef meal.

Wrong Protein Choices for Dogs

When you wish to feed your dogs the right proteins, you must identify the wrong ones so that you can eliminate them from the diet. Here are some wrong choices of proteins for your dogs.

Bad proteins for dogs are the ones that have lower biological values making them less ideal. They are as follows.

- Plant proteins such as corn, wheat and gluten that contain smaller amounts of protein are not good choices for dogs. Their digestive systems will not be able to process these and make it difficult for their bodies to adjust to these being fed raw. They also do not contain amino acids which further makes it unideal for dogs.

- Meat by-products are not ideal choices for your dog. They are the opposite of meat meals and will not contain any of the requisite nutrients required to keep your dog healthy. These refer to meats that have been stripped from animal carcasses and will not be healthy bits. They will hardly have any meat on them and include the likes of beaks, claws, horns, and hooves.

The rule is to stick with the real and natural meats and kick the artificial ones. Proteins derived from the real meats are sufficient to give your dog the much-needed energy and promote ideal muscle gain. It is a must for you to make the effort to find the healthiest meat available. Only high-quality meat should be fed as it can nourish their entire bodies leading to stronger muscles and healthier bones.

Chapter Twelve: Immunity Boosters For Dogs

If you want your dog to develop a strong immunity and stave off diseases then here are some foods to incorporate in their diet.

Fish Oil

The number one recommended immunity booster for dogs is fish oil. It contains a combination of Omega 3 and Omega 6 fatty acids that are both important to improve your dog's skin and coat health and bolster overall immunity. It helps to reduce inflammation and pain. But make sure you do not overfeed your dog fish oil, as it can cut into the vitamin E content in their system.

Vitamin E

Vitamin E plays a very important role in keeping your dog's heart health and immune system in top shape. It is also great for their skin, coat, eyes ,and muscles. Consult your vet to know the recommended amount for your dog.

Rosemary

Rosemary is high in iron, vitamins B6, and calcium that are required to keep your dog's muscles and bones strong. They also contain antioxidants needed to keep them healthy from the inside out. Adding just a little rosemary to their diet can make them appreciate their meals more and enhance good breath.

Biotin

Biotin deficiencies in dogs are not common but can affect a few owing to poor diet. The best way to tell is by examining the skin and coat. If it is dull and lifeless then it means there is a biotin deficiency. If they suffer from dry and itchy skin then it is best to give them a supplement to put an end to the issues. The best way to do so is by opening up a biotin capsule and sprinkling the contents over their meals.

Coconut Oil

Coconut oil is typically not a go-to for pet owners but its real benefits are often understated. It has antibacterial, antifungal and antiviral properties that are needed to keep your dog healthy. Coconut oil is known to enhance skin conditions, help with digestion and control illnesses such as diabetes. All you have to do is drizzle some virgin coconut oil over their meals.

Peppermint

Peppermint is a great choice for those looking to keep their dog's breath fresh and smelling good. Adding just a little can keep them healthy and their breaths fresh. It will also help to keep their digestive tract clean and reduce occurrences of nausea and flatulence.

Plain Yogurt

Plain yogurt that is not flavored and unsweetened can be a great source of calcium and probiotics for dogs. It can give your dog many gastrointestinal benefits and keep the digestive tract clean.

Vitamin C

Vitamin C is naturally produced in dog's bodies but it is still quite important to add it to their meals. Vitamin C can help to control certain conditions such as glaucoma and keep infections in check. Ask your dog's vet to recommend the right amount of vitamin C that should be included in their meals.

Pumpkin

Pumpkin is a great choice to add to your dog's meals if they are suffering from gastrointestinal issues. It contains an unusually high level of fiber, which can keep their systems clean and well maintained. The fiber can make it easier for them to eliminate without much effort. If you dog is having a little discomfort then puree a pumpkin and add it to the meal. Go for fresh pumpkin e and avoid the one that comes from cans. It is never an option to give your dog pumpkin pie filling.

Echinacea

Echinacea has been often used to treat illnesses in humans and its usefulness in treating illnesses in dogs has been proven over the years. Although only one study has been conducted on its usefulness, the results have been quite satisfactory and said to prevent respiratory illnesses in dogs.

Diatomaceous Earth

Diatomaceous Earth is an element commonly found in fossils of freshwater and marine organisms. There are two types including food grade and pool grade. You must make sure to use the food grade ones for your dog as the pool grade one can be toxic. It is fed to fight against parasites that can be inside the dog. It is also used to rub over the coat of the dog to control fleas, ticks and other insects that can infest their skin and coat. A little can be sprinkled in the areas where your pet usually sits or sleeps including the couch, carpet, and their bedding.

Chapter Thirteen: Types Of Raw Treats For Dogs

Raw treats for dogs are ideal to be fed when training them or appreciating them for some good work they have done. Here are some raw treats you can try.

Lamb Bones

One of the best types of treats includes lamb bones. Go for grass fed lamb bones that will make an excellent choice for gnawing.

Duck Necks

Duck necks are a good treat. Free-range duck necks can be given to your dog as a treat and can be quite a satisfying option.

Green Tripe

Green tripe is a great choice to treat your dogs. It is made of enzymes and contains good bacteria that are needed to keep your dog's stomach clean.

Venison Jerky Treats

Venison jerky treats are usually without any filters and can be broken into small bits that are perfect for your dogs as treats.

Vegetables

Vegetables such as carrots and beetroots are excellent treats. Cut them into bite-sized pieces to make it easier for your dogs to chew.

Fruits

Fruits such as bananas and apples can be given as treats.

Chapter Fourteen: Tips For Fresher Breath And Cleaner Teeth

It is essential for pet owners to pay attention to their dog's oral hygiene. Right from maintaining cleaner teeth to fresher breath, it is a must to feed them foods that can take care of these aspects. Here are some ingredients that can lend your dog fresher breath.

Probiotics

A common myth is that a dog's bad breath is a result of bad oral hygiene; however, this is not true. It can be a result of improper digestive health. Probiotics can be administered to keep good bacteria in their intestinal tract and promote better digestion. It will in turn lead to fresher breath and prevent formation of bad bacteria in their mouth.

Bones

Bones are a great choice not just to keep your dog busy but also keep their mouths clean. If you give them the right type of bones that are not too hard or too soft then they can brush against the surface of the plaque and reduce it considerably. It can be the same as brushing their teeth. Go for natural marrow bones that are fresh. Don't opt for frozen or processed marrow that is commercially packed to prolong the life of the product.

Food

An aspect that many people tend to overlook is the kind of food that is fed to dogs. It is important to feed them foods that are good for their overall health. It should be clean and fresh and suit their needs. If they suffer from digestive tract issues and conditions such as loose stools and gas then bad breath will be common. Go for natural raw meats and not by products.

Parsley and Mint

Both parsley and mint can help to keep your dog's mouth clean and free from odors. The chlorophyll content in parsley helps to keep your dog's breath clean. It freshens the breath and is easy to incorporate in their daily meals. All you have to do is cut it into small pieces and sprinkle it over the meals. The same goes for mint leaves. It is an inexpensive way to deodorize your dog's breath.

Coconut Oil

Coconut oil is a good ingredient to be used to control your dog's bad breath. It has properties that cannot only soothe an upset stomach but also heal any wounds that might be present inside the dog's mouth. Add one teaspoon of oil for every ten pounds of body weight. Also consider dipping parsley in coconut oil and feeding it to them so that they can chew on it and develop fresher breath.

Apple Cider Vinegar

Apple cider vinegar is a good choice to add to not just your dog's bowl of food but also the water he drinks to keep his breath fresh and mouth clean. Add about half or one teaspoon to the water and the same to his or her bowl of food.

Natural Treats

Natural treats also make an excellent choice to boost fresh breath and keep their teeth and gums healthy. Right from raw carrots to sweet potatoes, they can serve as natural toothbrush to keep the teeth clean and free from build-up.

If you feel like despite feeding them all these treats there is still a bad breath issue then it might indicate the presence of an undiagnosed illness. Take your dog to the vet to find out if there is an issue. In general, it should take not any more than a month for the bad breath issue to get sorted out.

Chapter:
20 Raw Food Recipes for Dogs

Portions for dogs: Feed the dog 2 to 3% of their body weight per day, depending on the weight of the dog. Start with a little and increase gradually.

Make portions accordingly.

1. Basic Raw Dog Food

Yields: Approximately 15.5 pounds

Ingredients:

- 11 pounds meat, chopped or minced
- 1.1 pounds par-cooked vegetables like carrots, green beans, peas, yam, celery, greens etc.
- 1.1 pounds organ meat

Power additions:

- 2-3 whole raw eggs
- 1 ½ tablespoons oil (choose from cod liver,

flax, primrose oil, hemp oil)
- 1-2 tablespoons kelp powder
- 3-4 cup oats (optional)

Method:

1. You can also use raw vegetables if you do not want to parboil the vegetables.
2. Add mincemeat, organ meat, vegetables, eggs (with shells), oil, kelp powder and oats into a mixing tub.
3. Make portions. Place each portion in separate bags or lunch boxes. Keep 1 bag in the refrigerator to use and rest of the bags in the freezer.
4. Use within for 2-3 weeks. Remove one bag from the freezer daily and place in the refrigerator to thaw.
5. Serve at room temperature or warm.

2. Standard Raw Food for Dogs

Yields: Approximately 23 pounds

Ingredients:

- 11 pounds fresh Irish chicken mince with 15% bone
- 1.1 pounds beef or mixture of beef and pork liver
- 1.1 pounds beef or mixture of beef and pork heart1.1 pounds beef or mixture of beef and pork kidney
- 1.1 pounds frozen vegetables (mixture of peas, green beans and carrots) or any other vegetables of your dog's preference
- 5.5 pounds fresh Irish red meat with 15% bone (duck, beef or pork)
- 2 free range eggs

Power additions:

- 2-3 pounds cooked or soaked porridge oats or boiled brown rice or boiled potatoes
- 2 ½ tablespoons cod liver oil

Method:

1. Add mincemeat, organ meat, vegetables, eggs (with shells), oil and oats into a mixing tub. Mix until well combined.

2. Make portions. Place each portion in separate bags or lunch boxes. Keep 1 bag in the refrigerator to use and rest of the bags in the freezer.

3. Use within for 2-3 weeks. Remove one bag from the freezer daily and place in the refrigerator to thaw.

4. Serve at room temperature or warm.

3. Active/Puppy Raw Dog Food

Yields: Approximately 24.25 pounds

Ingredients:

- 5.5 pounds fresh Irish chicken mince with 15% bone
- 5.5 pounds fresh Irish duck mince with 15% bone
- 2.2 pounds beef or mixture of beef and pork liver
- 1.1 pounds beef or mixture of beef and pork heart
- 1.1 pounds beef or mixture of beef and pork kidney
- 2.2 pounds frozen vegetables (mixture of peas, green beans and carrots) or any other vegetables of your dog's preference
- 5.5 pounds fatty Irish beef mince
- 2.2 pounds boiled brown rice
- 3 free range eggs

Method:

1. Add mincemeat, organ meat, vegetables,

eggs, oil and boiled rice into a mixing tub. Mix until well combined.

2. Make portions. Place each portion in separate bags or lunch boxes. Keep 1 bag in the refrigerator to use and rest of the bags in the freezer.

3. Use within for 2-3 weeks. Remove one bag from the freezer daily and place in the refrigerator to thaw.

4. Serve at room temperature or warm.

Note: To increase the calories in the food, replace chicken mince with equivalent amount of duck mince. You can also increase the quantity of brown rice.

To reduce calories, replace red meat with equivalent amount of chicken or fish or turkey mince.

4. Chicken and Carrots for Beginners

Yields: Approximately 25.3 pounds

Ingredients:

- 6.6 pounds chicken heart and liver
- 11 pounds chicken thighs or breasts
- 3.3 pounds ground chicken bone
- 2.2 pounds organic green beans, finely chopped
- 2.2 pounds organic carrots, finely chopped
- 3 chicken eggs, lightly boiled

Method:

1. Add chicken thighs or breasts, ground chicken bone, organ meat, beans, carrots, eggs (with shells) into a mixing tub. Mix until well combined.

2. Make portions. Place each portion in separate bags or lunch boxes. Keep 1 bag in the refrigerator to use and rest of the bags in the freezer.

3. Use within for 2-3 weeks. Remove one bag from the freezer daily and place in the refrigerator to thaw.

4. Serve at room temperature or warm.

5. Beef and Greens for beginners

Yields: Approximately 28 pounds

Ingredients:

- 11 pounds ground, cheek or stewing beef
- 3.3 pounds beef tail bones
- 6.6 pounds beef hearts and liver
- 2.2 pounds celery, finely chopped
- 1.1 pounds collard greens, finely chopped
- 2.2 pounds green apples, finely chopped
- 4 pounds kale, discard hard ribs and stems, finely chopped
- 3 chicken eggs, lightly boiled

Method:

1. Add meat, organ meat, tailbones, eggs (with its shells), apples, celery, collard greens and kale into a mixing tub. Mix until well combined.

2. Make portions. Place each portion in separate bags or lunch boxes. Keep 1 bag in the refrigerator to use and rest of the bags in the freezer.

3. Use within for 2-3 weeks. Remove one bag from the freezer daily and place in the refrigerator to thaw.

4. Serve at room temperature or warm.

6. Chicken and Greens for beginners

Yields: Approximately 27- 28 pounds

Ingredients:

- 11 pounds chicken thighs, breasts, chopped into pieces
- 3.3 pounds ground chicken bones
- 6.6 pounds chicken hearts and liver
- 2.2 pounds celery, finely chopped
- 1.1 pounds broccoli, finely chopped
- 2.2 pounds carrots, finely chopped
- 2.2 pounds spinach, finely chopped
- 3 chicken eggs, lightly boiled

Method:

1. Add chicken thighs or breasts, ground chicken bones, organ meat, eggs (with its shells), carrots, celery, spinach and broccoli into a mixing tub. Mix until well combined.
2. Make portions. Place each portion in separate bags or lunch boxes. Keep 1 bag in the refrigerator to use and rest of the bags in the freezer.

3. Use within for 2-3 weeks. Remove one bag from the freezer daily and place in the refrigerator to thaw.

4. Serve at room temperature or warm.

7. Turkey and Greens for beginners

Yields: Approximately 27 pounds

Ingredients:

- 8 pounds turkey thighs, breasts or tenderloins, chopped into pieces
- 3.3 pounds ground turkey necks
- 6.6 pounds turkey hearts and liver
- 2.2 pounds turkey gizzard
- 2.2 pounds lettuce, finely chopped
- 2.2 pounds yams or sweet potatoes, finely chopped
- 2.2 pounds zucchini, finely chopped

Method:

1. Add turkey thighs or breasts or, organ meat, gizzard, necks lettuce, yam or sweet potato into a mixing tub. Mix until well combined.
2. Make portions. Place each portion in separate bags or lunch boxes. Keep 1 bag in the refrigerator to use and rest of the bags in the freezer.

3. Use within for 2-3 weeks. Remove one bag from the freezer daily and place in the refrigerator to thaw.

4. Serve at room temperature or warm.

8. Sweet Turkey for beginners

Yields: Approximately 27 pounds

Ingredients:

- 6.6 pounds turkey hearts and liver
- 11 pounds turkey thighs, breasts or tenderloins, chopped into pieces
- 2.2 pounds yams or sweet potatoes, finely chopped
- 2.2 pounds cooked chickpeas1 cup dried eggs
- 2.2 pounds cranberries
- 2.2 pounds green beans

Method:

1. Add turkey thighs, breasts or tenderloins, organ meat, chickpeas, green beans, cranberries, yam or sweet potato and dried eggs into a mixing tub. Mix until well combined.
2. Make portions. Place each portion in separate bags or lunch boxes. Keep 1 bag in the refrigerator to use and rest of the bags in the freezer.
3. Use within for 2-3 weeks. Remove one bag

from the freezer daily and place in the refrigerator to thaw.

4. Serve at room temperature or warm.

9. Chicken and Beef Delight

Yields: Approximately 27 pounds

Ingredients:

- 5.5 pounds chicken thighs, breasts, chopped into pieces
- 3.3 pounds ground chicken bones
- 6.6 pounds beef hearts and liver
- 5.5 pounds ground beef, cheek or stewing
- 2.2 pounds yams or sweet potatoes, finely cubed
- 2.2 pounds broccoli, finely chopped
- 1.1 pounds sunflower meal
- 1.1 pounds linseed meal

Method:

1. Add chicken thighs or breasts, ground chicken bones, ground beef, organ meat, yam, broccoli, sunflower meal and linseed meal into a mixing tub. Mix until well combined.

2. Make portions. Place each portion in separate bags or lunch boxes. Keep 1 bag in the

refrigerator to use and rest of the bags in the freezer.

3. Use within for 2-3 weeks. Remove one bag from the freezer daily and place in the refrigerator to thaw.

4. Serve at room temperature or warm.

10. Chicken, Turkey and Fish Delight

Yields: Approximately 25 pounds

Ingredients:

- 11 pounds herring, chopped into pieces
- 3.3 pounds ground chicken bones and turkey bones
- 6.6 pounds chicken and turkey hearts and liver
- 2.2 pounds cooked chickpeas
- 2.2 pounds spinach, finely chopped
- 3 chicken eggs, lightly boiled

Method:

1. Add herring, ground chicken and turkey bones, organ meat, eggs (with its shells), chickpeas and spinach into a mixing tub. Mix until well combined.

2. Make portions. Place each portion in separate bags or lunch boxes. Keep 1 bag in the refrigerator to use and rest of the bags in the freezer.

3. Use within for 2-3 weeks. Remove one bag from the freezer daily and place in the refrigerator to thaw.

4. Serve at room temperature or warm.

11. Raw Food Cakes

Yields: Approximately 24 pounds

Ingredients:

- 4 cups brown or white rice
- 8 -10 cups water or unsalted chicken broth without onion or garlic
- 4 large yams, steamed or baked, mashed
- 4 cups pumpkin puree
- 1 pound green beans, finely chopped
- 1 pound snap peas
- 2 large bunches parsley, chopped
- 2 -3 dozens egg shells, baked in an oven until dry
- 18 eggs, lightly poached, cooled
- 2 cups natural peanut butter
- 1 1/3 cups nutritional yeast
- 2 cups flax meal
- 2 cups raw pumpkin seeds or almonds, ground

- 2 cups rolled oats (optional)
- 2 cups rolled oats, ground (optional)
- 1 cup olive oil
- 1 cup rose hips, dried, ground in a coffee grinder
- 2 peaches, pitted, chopped
- 2 pears, cored, peeled, chopped
- 4 plums, pitted, chopped
- 8 large apples, cored, chopped
- 16 large carrots, finely chopped
- ½ head cabbage, finely chopped (do not grind)
- 2 heads broccoli, finely chopped
- 12 celery stalks, finely chopped
- 2 large zucchini or summer squash, finely chopped
- 1 pound cranberries
- 1 pound blueberries

Method:

1. Add rice and broth into a saucepan or rice cooker and cook the rice.

2. Meanwhile, add the vegetables (except cabbage) or fruits that need to be finely chopped if desired in the food processor. Process until finely chopped.

3. Gather all the ingredients and add into a mixing tub. Mix until well combined.

4. Line 4-5 baking sheets with parchment paper. Make cakes of the mixture and place on the baking sheet, next to each other.

5. Place the baking trays in the freezer and freeze until firm.

6. Make portions. Place each portion in separate bags or lunch boxes. Keep 1 bag in the refrigerator to use and rest of the bags in the freezer.

7. Use within for 2-3 weeks. Remove one bag from the freezer daily and place in the refrigerator to thaw.

8. Serve at room temperature or warm.

Note: Some of the fruit or vegetables mentioned in the recipe may be seasonal so you can add substitute it for some other fruit or vegetable that your dog prefers. You can also make changes suiting to your dog's preference.

12. Meat, Fruit and Vegetable Patties

Yields: Approximately 6 pounds

Ingredients:

- ½ pound chicken livers
- 5 pounds ground beef
- 2 small apples, cored, chopped
- 2 carrots, chopped
- 1 cup baby spinach, chopped
- 1 cup plain yogurt
- 2 tablespoons olive oil
- 4 whole eggs, lightly boiled
- 2 tablespoons ground flaxseed

Method:

1. Add fruit and vegetables into the food processor bowl and pulse until the mixture is finely chopped.

2. Add chicken liver, yogurt, olive oil, eggs and flaxseed and pulse until well incorporated.

3. Remove the mixture into a mixing tub. Add beef and mix until well incorporated.

4. Shape into patties of about 3-4 inches diameter.

5. Line 2 baking sheets with parchment paper. Place the patties on the baking sheet, next to each other.

6. Place the baking trays in the freezer and freeze until firm.

7. Make portions. Place each portion in separate bags or lunch boxes. Keep 1 bag in the refrigerator to use and rest of the bags in the freezer.

8. Use within for 2-3 weeks. Remove one bag from the freezer daily and place in the refrigerator to thaw.

9. Serve at room temperature or warm.

13. Lamb/Beef, Vegetable and Fruit for Small Breed Dogs up to 17.5 Pounds

Yields: Approximately 2-2 ½ pounds

Ingredients:

- 1.1 pounds lamb or beef, chopped
- 2 apples, cored, chopped
- 3 cups pumpkin or squash, chopped
- 2 large carrots, chopped (about 2 cups)
- ½ cup frozen peas, thawed
- 1 1/3 cups brown or basmati rice
- 3 cups water or unsalted broth without onion or garlic
- 2 teaspoons fish oil
- 8 teaspoons sunflower oil

Other ingredients: To be added at each feed

- 1 Cenovis tablets (zinc tablets)
- 1/8 teaspoon iodized salt
- 1 trace nutrients copper plus tablet (2 mg)

- 1 Centrum Advance multivitamin / multi-mineral supplement

Method:

1. Add rice, broth or water and pumpkin into a saucepan. Cook until very tender. Turn off the heat and cool completely.

2. Add meat, apple, pumpkin, carrots, peas, rice, fish oil and sunflower oil, into a mixing tub. Mix until well combined.

3. Make portions. Place each portion in separate bags or lunch boxes. Keep 1 bag in the refrigerator to use and rest of the bags in the freezer.

4. Use within for 2-3 weeks. Remove one bag from the freezer daily and place in the refrigerator to thaw.

5. Serve at room temperature or warm.

6. Add Cenovis tablet, salt, copper plus tablet and Centrum in each feed while serving.

14. Beef and Eggs

Yields: Approximately 12 pounds.

Ingredients:

- 5 pounds raw ground beef
- 7-8 cups cooked white rice, cooled
- 9 hard boiled eggs, with shells, cooled
- Dinovite daily dog supplement, follow the instructions on the package and use accordingly or use 1 tablespoon per cup of the recipe
- 2 tubes LickOchops

Method:

1. Add ground beef, white rice and eggs, into a mixing tub. Mix until well combined.

2. Make portions. Place each portion in separate bags or lunch boxes. Keep 1 bag in the refrigerator to use and rest of the bags in the freezer.

3. Use within for 2-3 weeks. Remove one bag from the freezer daily and place in the refrigerator to thaw.

4. Serve at room temperature or warm.

5. Follow the instructions on the packages of Dinovite and LickOchops and add into the portion while serving.

Note: Please do not give it to your dog without Dinovite and LickOchops.

15. Meatballs

Serving size:

3-5 meatballs (1 cup size each) per day for large breed (50-100 pounds dog), depending on the weight of the dog

2-3 meatballs (1 cup size each) per day for medium breed (20-40 pounds dog), depending on the weight of the dog

1-2 meatballs (½ cup size each) per day for small breed (1-10 pounds dog), depending on the weight of the dog

Ingredients:

- 4 pounds frozen fish fillets like mackerel or whiting
- ½ -1 pound beef liver
- 2 cans Alaskan wild pink salmon
- 2-6 eggs (optional)
- 1 large carrot, cut into small pieces (about 1 cup), cooked
- 1 cup broccoli, cut into small florets, cooked
- 1 cup yam, cut into small pieces, cooked

- 1 large apple, cored, cut into small pieces
- 1 cup raw pumpkin seeds (pepitas)
- 4 tablespoons dried oregano
- 4 tablespoons dried parsley
- 4 tablespoons honey
- 4 tablespoons Thorvin kelp powder
- 4 tablespoons turmeric powder
- 2 cups cooked oatmeal or barley or brown rice (optional)

Method:

1. Using a meat grinder, grind frozen fish, liver, carrots, broccoli, yam, apple and pepitas into a large bowl.

2. Add salmon, eggs, oregano, parsley, honey, oatmeal if using and kelp powder. Mix well.

3. Make meatballs and place on a baking sheet. Freeze until firm.

4. Make portions. Place each portion in separate bags or lunch boxes. Keep 1 bag in the refrigerator to use and rest of the bags in the freezer.

5. Use within for 2-3 weeks. Remove one bag from the freezer daily and place in the refrigerator to thaw.

6. Serve at room temperature or warm.

16. Chicken and Fish Exotica

Yields: Approximately 35 pounds

Ingredients:

- 5 pounds chicken hearts
- 20 pounds chicken necks without skin
- 2 ½ -5 pounds chicken liver
- 4 cans Alaskan wild pink salmon (optional)
- 1-2 ½ pounds carrots, cut into small pieces
- 1 small beet, cut into small pieces
- 1 pound spinach or any other greens your dog prefers
- 2 cups red cabbage, finely chopped
- 1 apple, cored, cut into small pieces
- ½ cup raw pumpkin seeds (pepitas)

Other ingredients: Use 2-3 of these

- 2-6 raw eggs
- ½ cup tahini
- 1 cup extra virgin olive oil

- 4-8 tablespoons dried oregano
- 4-8 tablespoons dried parsley
- 2 tablespoons honey
- 2-4 tablespoons Thorvin kelp powder
- 2 tablespoons turmeric powder
- 1000 mg vitamin C powder

Method:

1. Using a meat grinder, grind chicken heart, chicken liver, chicken neck, carrots, beet, spinach, red cabbage, apple and pepitas into a mixing tub.
2. Add rest of the ingredients and mix until well combined.
3. Make portions. Place each portion in separate bags or lunch boxes. Keep 1 bag in the refrigerator to use and rest of the bags in the freezer.
4. Use within for 2-3 weeks. Remove one bag from the freezer daily and place in the refrigerator to thaw.
5. Serve at room temperature or warm.

17. Pupcakes – Christmas Pudding for Doggies

Yields: 4 servings

Ingredients:

- 1 pound raw beef mince
- 1 cup raw pumpkin, puree
- 1 cup raw carrot, puree
- 2 tablespoons extra virgin coconut oil
- ¼ cup ground flaxseeds
- ¼ cup ground sunflower seeds
- Coconut flour to dust
- 4 raspberries, to garnish
- 4 blueberries, to garnish

Method:

1. Add raw pumpkin cubes into the food processor and process until smooth. Measure out 1 cup of the pureed pumpkin and add into a mixing bowl.

2. Add raw carrot cubes into the food processor and process until smooth. Measure out 1 cup

of the pureed carrot and add into the bowl of pumpkin.

3. Add beef mince and mix until well combined.

4. Add coconut oil and mix until well combined.

5. Add ground flax seeds and sunflower seeds and stir until well combined. You can use your hands to combine the mixture.

6. Fill into 4 ramekins or teacups. Press it well onto the bottom of the cups. Chill for 30-40 minutes.

7. Remove from the refrigerator and invert on to a plate. Tap the bottom of the cup to loosen the pudding.

8. Dust the pudding with coconut flour. Garnish with a raspberry and a blueberry on each pudding and serve.

9. Place individual portions in separate containers and place in the refrigerator.

18. Fruit Parfait for Dogs

Makes: 16 servings of ¼ cup each

Ingredients:

- 1 cup plain, nonfat yogurt
- 1 cup blueberries, chopped
- 1 cup strawberries, chopped
- 1 cup applesauce, unsweetened

Method:

1. Add yogurt, blueberries, strawberries and applesauce into a blender and blend until smooth.
2. Transfer into an airtight container. Refrigerate until use. It can last for 7 days.
3. Remove ¼ cup of the parfait and serve. Refrigerate the remaining.

19. Frozen Strawberry and Banana Smoothie Treat

Makes: Approximately 12 molds

Ingredients:

- 2 bags frozen strawberries (16 ounces each)
- 2 bananas, sliced
- 6 tablespoons honey
- 3 cups plain, low fat Greek yogurt
- ½ cup skim milk

Method:

1. Add strawberries, yogurt, banana, honey, yogurt and skim milk into a blender and blend until smooth.
2. Pour into molds and freeze until firm.
3. Remove from the molds and serve.
4. Transfer the remaining treats into Ziploc bags and freeze.

20. Pupsicles

Makes: Approximately 12 molds

Ingredients:

- 2 cups frozen strawberries
- 2 cups frozen blueberries
- 2 cups nonfat plain yogurt
- Water, as required
- ½ cup plain peanut butter

Method:

1. Add strawberries, blueberries, yogurt, water and peanut butter into a blender. Blend until smooth.

2. Pour into Dog bone molds. You can also use ice trays.

3. Freeze until firm.

Remove from mold and serve. Transfer the remaining pupsicles into Ziploc bags and freeze until firm.

Conclusion

I thank you once again for choosing this book and hope you had a good time reading it.

The main aim of this book was to educate you on the basics of the raw diet for dogs and how you can transition your dog into the diet. As you can see, it is quite easy to do so if you follow the right steps. Your dog will be happier and healthier and be able to live a long and healthy life. But make sure you allow him or her to adjust to the diet and transition them phase-by-phase.

I urge you to go through the book once again so that you know exactly what it takes to transition your dog to adopt the raw food diet and the health benefits that it can provide. Remember to remain consistent and not fall back into the habit of feeding them kibble. Maintain a journal to record what you feed them and their overall progress.

I hope you have a good time feeding your dog a raw diet and they have fun too!

References:

https://sciencebasedmedicine.org/the-top-ten-pet-supplements-do-they-work/

http://theconversation.com/should-you-feed-your-pet-raw-meat-the-real-risks-of-a-traditional-dog-diet-90271

https://www.dogster.com/dog-food/dog-nutrition-nutrients-dogs-need

https://keepthetailwagging.com/alternative-proteins-for-a-dog-with-a-beef-or-chicken-allergy/

https://www.rexpetfood.com/en/benefits-of-lysine-in-dogs-food/

https://livesimply.me/2014/08/01/ultimate-guide-finding-grass-fed-meat/

https://www.couchwolves.com/latest-news/2018/2/25/prey-model-raw-diet

https://www.dog-obedience-training-review.com/barf-raw-dog-food-diet.html

https://therawfeedingcommunity.com/2018/03/11/how-much-does-it-cost-to-feed-raw/

https://www.dogsnaturallymagazine.com/10-reasons-to-feed-vegetables-for-dogs/

https://www.dogsnaturallymagazine.com/raw-meat-diet-for-dogs-7-myths-you-wont-believe/

https://bullymax.com/best-protein-sources-dogs/

https://iheartdogs.com/12-things-you-can-sneak-into-your-dogs-food-to-boost-their-health/

https://keepthetailwagging.com/will-raw-feeding-help-my-dog-lose-weight/

https://www.chewy.com/petcentral/health-wellness-6-ways-to-naturally-freshen-your-dogs-breath/

Printed in Great Britain
by Amazon